The Ultimate Paleo Desserts

Satisfy Your Sweet Tooth With Over 100 Quick and Easy Paleo Dessert Recipes and Paleo Baking Recipes

Emma Rose

Table Of Contents

Introduction

I want to thank you for purchasing this book!

This book contains 100 Paleo dessert and baking recipes on how to prepare delectable desserts without sacrificing your health.

All my life I've had a sweet tooth. I would even go as far as to say that I had a sugar addiction! Over the last few years my sugar addiction got worse: I had dessert multiple times a day and every day (I guess being a Foods teacher didn't help much). I would joke with people by telling them that I had my servings of vegetables for the day in chocolate...except, I still didn't have the vegetables. It got pretty bad. I knew I hated eating that much dessert but I couldn't stop. I would eat one Ferrero Rocher and then go back for another. As I walked back to the treats, I would pass the mirror and think to myself, "I don't need to have this chocolate. But, ah, what the heck, I don't care." In the end, I'd have about 6 Ferrero Rocher in addition to the other treats I had earlier that day.

Finally, I had to take the huge tray of Ferrero Rocher to school to give to my students on Valentine's Day. There was no way I could eat the other 30 myself. Eating all this sugar caused a huge war within me. I knew that my extreme sugar eating was unhealthy for me but I didn't want to stop. I loved it too much. As a result, I wrestled between the ideal of where I wanted to be and the reality of where I was. I knew I had the discipline to say no to other things, so why couldn't I say no to chocolate?

I eventually came to the point where I was starting to get fed up with not feeling well. I had a lot of chronic pain in my neck and I was constantly tired. I knew that sugar was irritating the problem and causing inflammation in my body. At was starting to reach the breaking point. Ultimately, I chose to go off of sugar for at least three weeks to break the habit I had created for myself. It was seriously a miracle to stay consistent with my goal because I really didn't want to give up my favorite desserts.

Shortly after my decision to go off of sugar, I had a miscarriage. Experiencing the loss catapulted me into a massive journey to find health and proper nutrition. I did a live blood analysis with a naturopath to discover what was contributing to the terrible ways I was feeling. Seeing all the garbage I had in my blood forced me to go off of dairy, corn, oats, and wheat. I was left wondering, "What the heck am I going to eat? That stuff is in everything!"

Consequently, I stumbled upon the Paleo Free Diet. It was the most relevant diet to what I was trying to accomplish. I was able to find things to eat for breakfast, lunch and dinner. But desserts were a whole other story. I felt like something was missing and I couldn't put my finger on it. The best I could come up with was apple slices dipped in almond butter: hardly satisfying. Paleo desserts ended up being the by-product of my search to find something, anything that I could enjoy.

I encourage you to make that switch to healthier and happier desserts with the hundred delicious and irresistible recipes presented in this book. You don't need to follow the same extremity that I did. But if you are taking the Paleo Free Diet seriously, then you may find the same void of sweets in your life too. Cutting out all the processed foods and going back to the basics really does clear up the body and help it function better. I've seen the changes in my own life as hard as it's been to make those changes. You, too, can make the changes necessary and still have your sweets along the way!

6

Thank you again for purchasing this book. I hope you enjoy the recipes. Experiment with them and make substitutions to suit your needs. Please take some time to stop by and LIKE our Facebook page:

https://www.facebook.com/joypublishing

With gratitude,

Emma Rose

Chapter 1

Brief History of Paleo Free Diet

The Sweet Effects

Why do you love sweet food? Why do you crave for more of that dessert so much? Your anatomy would tell you that sweet foods would cause the release of dopamine in the part of the brain that is associated with motivation and reward. Not only that, but studies show that sweets also produce an increased level of serotonin. Serotonin gives you that feeling of happiness and wellbeing. That's why it is better to give a box of chocolates when you want the person to be in a good mood.

Unfortunately, the quote you can't have your cake and eat it too applies here. The bad effects that sugar brings are common knowledge. The number one disease is diabetes. People are aware of diabetes and its complications. That is why even when you intensely crave for that delicious dessert, you try to control your urges and settle for nothing instead. Well, that is if your self-control is in good condition. More often than not, people would rather risk the medical condition and eat that sweet thing with all their heart.

I have had many slip ups in my own life. I went two months without chocolate...can you believe it? Then Easter came. I found that if I gave myself an inch, I would take a mile. Eating chocolate quickly got out of control. I rebelled because I was strict for so long. You may find yourself in the same situation and find it hard to balance the sugar cravings. Once the sugar cravings are there, your body craves more and then a vicious cycle begins.

What is Paleo Free Diet?

Here is Paleo desserts to the rescue! You can have your cake and eat it too, literally. And not just cake only but lots more! Paleo is known by many names such as the cavemen diet, stone age diet and hunter-gatherer diet, to name a few. The concept behind this diet follows that of the Paleolithic era before the development of agriculture. This type of diet is still very young, only less than fifty years. However, more in depth researches and studies are being conducted to increase the information and knowledge on this diet.

The results of previous studies on the Paleo Free Diet reveal an improvement in health to the people involved. This is attributed to the fact that no processed foods and additives are included. Foods that were not available during the Paleolithic time such as dairy products, salt, sugar and grains are also not included in the preparation of the Paleo Free Diet. These ingredients are known to cause some of these diseases indirectly such as hypertension, diabetes, strokes, obesity and other heart problems. The same goes for the Paleo desserts. They are as delicious as the desserts that are found in the market but healthier.

You will notice that sugar shows up in the form of honey, maple syrup or chocolate. It can be argued that these sources are natural compared to the refined sugar which is a by-product of our industrialization and modern world. The history of chocolate dates back to the ancient Mayans who used the cacao pods as a form of currency. You can be the judge as to whether you want to include these foods in your diet. When it comes to chocolate, I prefer organic fair trade chocolate made from cacao powder. Cacao powder is more unrefined and unprocessed compared to cocoa powder.

There are a hundred recipes here guaranteed to satisfy your sweet tooth by using these prehistoric ingredients free of additives and processed foods. Are you ready to satisfy your cravings? Here are the simple and easy to follow recipes that you would surely fall in love with.

Chapter 2 – Chocolatiest at its Best!

Who doesn't love chocolate? Here are 31 Paleo desserts with yummy chocolate as the main ingredient. Dairy free chocolates are preferred. And half of these recipes do not even need an oven to do them. Let's do the oven-*less* desserts first.

1.   ***Brownie Magic***

This recipe is super quick and only involves 3 common ingredients: cocoa powder, dates and walnuts.

Ingredients:
1 tablespoon cocoa powder
1 cup dates (softened in water first)
1 cup walnuts

Procedure:
Put the three ingredients into a blender and blend until smooth. Adjust the cocoa powder to taste. Once satisfied, roll the mixture into small balls. You'll have a brownie ready to munch anytime – morning, noon or night. Keep stored in refrigerator.

2. *The 3 C's Dessert*

These basic ingredients start with the letter C – chocolates, coffee and coconut butter.

Ingredients:
½ cup coconut butter, melted
1 tablespoon ground coffee
3 tablespoon 100% cocoa powder
½ teaspoon honey

Procedure:
Combine and mix thoroughly the coconut butter, ground coffee, cocoa powder, and honey. Lightly grease an ice cube tray with 1 tablespoon coconut oil. Then spoon the mixture and place them in the ice cube tray. Leave the ice cube tray in the freezer for 5 hours. Remove the tray from the freezer 15 minutes before serving.

3.   *Dairy Free Delight Part 1*

The main mixture would be done like this.

Ingredients:
2 cans (24 ounces) pure coconut milk
¼ cup cocoa powder
¼ teaspoon sweetener of choice
2 ounces unsweetened chocolate
1.5 tablespoon pure vanilla extract

Procedure:
Heat the coconut milk and cocoa powder in a medium saucepan on low-medium heat. Add the sweetener of your choice, unsweetened chocolate and pure vanilla extract. Allow the chocolate to melt and remove from heat. Let it cool and then place in the refrigerator for at least four hours. Remove from refrigerator and serve cool.

4.   *Dairy Free Delight Part 2*

Follow the same procedure in Part 1 but instead of serving it as it is, put the cooled mixture into an ice cream maker. Follow the manufacturer's instruction. Afterwards, you may want to top it with fresh fruit. Serve immediately. Or you may want to try Part 3 of this.

5.   *Dairy Free Delight Part 3*

A different version of Part 2 would be instead of serving it, put it back in the freezer for another hour (right after the coffee and talks would be great). The ice cream would be firmer. And the guests would be happier.

6.   *Dairy Free Delight Part 4*

Place the cooled mixture into popsicle molds and freeze for 4 hours. And that's it! This treat is great for kids and great for adults who are forever young.

7.   *Chunky Choco*

Ingredients:
6 ounces unsweetened chocolate
½ teaspoon vanilla
1/8 teaspoon sweetener of choice

Procedure:
Melt unsweetened chocolate using a double boiler. Make sure that the chocolate is completely melted. Remove from heat and continue stirring the chocolate while you add vanilla and sweetener of your choice. Place in a pan and let it set in the refrigerator for 30-45 minutes. You can cut into squares or let the kids design their own chunky chocolate.

8.   *Apple Chocolate on a Stick*

Insert a stick through the core of the apple (children, let the adults do this). Melt a bar of dark chocolate. When the chocolate is fully melted, dip the apple. Put in the refrigerator for 20 minutes to set. You can eat it as is or let the kids be more creative and add some toppings prior to placing it on the refrigerator.

9.   *Sixty Seconds Dessert*

Ingredients:
2 tablespoon coconut milk
1 tablespoon unsweetened cocoa powder
2 tablespoon coconut butter
¾ teaspoon pure vanilla extract
2 servings of sweetener

Procedure:

In a small bowl, add the following ingredients: coconut milk, unsweetened cocoa powder, coconut butter, pure vanilla extract and sweetener. Use the back of the spoon to blend it until smooth. That's it!

10.   ***Dark Chocolate Pudding***

Ingredients:
1 egg, beaten
½ ripe avocado
¼ cup coconut milk
2 tablespoon cacao powder
1 tablespoon coffee
1 pinch salt
1 pinch cinnamon powder
1 scoop vanilla flavored whey protein powder
0.35 ounces raw hazelnuts
2 tablespoon unsweetened shredded coconut

Procedure:
Put beaten egg, avocado and coconut milk into a blender or food processor and blend until smooth. Add cacao powder, coffee, salt, cinnamon powder and vanilla flavored whey protein powder. Blend until smooth again. Add raw hazelnuts and unsweetened shredded coconut and let it spin until the hazelnuts are turned into small pieces. Serve immediately or refrigerate before serving. You can top it with more tiny pieces hazelnut if you want.

11.   *10 Minutes No-bake Cookies*

You could also call this the salted caramel chocolate chunk cookies, whichever fits you.

Ingredients:
1 ½ cups sugar (try date or coconut sugar)
½ cup coconut milk
½ cup coconut oil
2 teaspoon vanilla extract
½ teaspoon sea salt
1 cup flake coconut
2/3 cup chocolate chunks or chips

Procedure:
In a saucepan, combine the following ingredients: sugar, coconut milk and coconut oil. Constantly stir while you bring it to boil. After 2-3 minutes of boiling (again, stir continuously- you don't want caramel to stick), remove from heat and add vanilla extract, sea salt and flake coconut. Add chocolate chunks or chips and stir softly. Set it in a pan and let it set for 2-3 hours. You can cut the cookies into shapes that you like.

12.   *Chocolate Madness*

Make chocolate cookies using the 10 Minutes No Bake Cookies. Place on a plate and add a small scoop of homemade chocolate ice cream. Top with chocolate chips. Serve!

13.   *Choco Fudge*

Ingredients:
¼ cup cocoa butter
¼ cup coconut oil
½ cup coconut butter
1 tablespoon honey
¼ serving of sweetener
¼ cup cocoa powder
1 teaspoon vanilla

Procedure:
In a pan with low heat, melt the cocoa butter. Add the cocoa butter, coconut oil and coconut butter. Use a whisk to mix. Add the honey, sweetener, cocoa powder and vanilla and gently whisk. Make sure that everything is properly mixed. There should be no lumps. Do not overheat. Place in an 8" by 8" pan lined with parchment paper and refrigerate for 1-2 hours. Cut according to your preference.

14.   *Chocolate Custard Delight*

Ingredients:
1 can coconut milk
1 cup dark chocolate
1 teaspoon vanilla

Procedure:
In a saucepan over low-medium heat, combine coconut milk and dark chocolate. Mix with a whisk until chocolate is melted. Add

vanilla. Pour into smaller glasses and let it set in the refrigerator. Top it with fresh fruit.

15.   *Strawberry Coated Chocolates*

Melt a bar of dark chocolate by using a double broiler. Dip as many strawberries as you want. Serve immediately.

16. *Cookie Topper*

Ingredients:
3 tablespoon coconut milk
2 tablespoon coconut cream, concentrate
½ tablespoon pure vanilla extract
3 tablespoon cacao powder
3 servings of sweetener

Procedure:
In a bowl, combine coconut milk and coconut cream concentrate. Add pure vanilla extract, cacao powder and sweetener. Whisk until the mixture is very creamy. Place on top of any homemade cookie. Add ice cream if you like.

17. *Choco Fruit Dip*

Ingredients:
1 cup coconut
1 teaspoon vanilla
2 ripe bananas
2 teaspoon coconut flour
1 ½ tablespoon unsweetened cocoa powder

Procedure:
Place into a food processor or blender the following ingredients: coconut, vanilla, bananas and coconut flour. Blend until smooth. Add the unsweetened cocoa powder. Serve with a platter of strawberries or apples.

18.   *Black Forest Shake*

Ingredients:
1 cup pitted cherries
2 tablespoon unsweetened cocoa powder
1 cup coconut milk

Procedure:
Place in a blender pitted cherries, unsweetened cocoa powder, coconut milk. Whir until smooth. Top with toasted shredded coconut.

19.   *Choco Thickshake*

Ingredients:
4 dried dates
½ banana
1/3 cup hazelnuts
1 teaspoon honey
1 tablespoon cocoa powder
1 tablespoon cacao powder
1 cup coconut milk
3-4 ice cubes
¼ cup strong coffee

Procedure:
Place in a blender the following ingredients: dried dates, banana, hazelnuts, honey, cocoa powder, cacao powder, coconut milk, ice, and strong coffee. Whir and wow! A refreshing drink and dessert rolled into one.

20.   *Minty Chocolate Shake*

Ingredients:
1 tablespoon maple syrup
8 fresh mint leaves
1 ½ tablespoon cocoa powder
1 cup coconut cream
3-4 ice cubes

Procedure:
Combine and blend the following: maple syrup, mint leaves, cocoa powder, coconut cream and ice cubes. Whir until smooth!

21.   *Strawberry with Chocolate Chips Ice Cream*

Ingredients:
5-7 frozen strawberries
½ cup coconut milk
1 teaspoon vanilla extract

Procedure:
Blend frozen strawberries, coconut milk and vanilla extract. Place in the freezer for one hour. Top with chocolate chips. Then it's ready to be served!

22.   *Yummy Pudding*

Ingredients:
1 egg
¼ cup coconut milk
2 tablespoon cacao powder
1 scoop chocolate flavored whey protein powder
1 pinch sea salt
1 pinch cinnamon powder

Procedure:
Blend until smooth the following: egg, coconut milk, cacao powder, chocolate flavored whey protein powder, sea salt and cinnamon powder. Refrigerate for at least 30 minutes. Top with nuts, if you wish.

23.   *Chocolate-Raspberry Layered Delight*

In a small glass, pour melted chocolate. Place ¼ cup raspberries. Pour melted chocolate again and a spoonful of almond butter. Place 2 sliced bananas on top and finish with a melted chocolate.

24.   *Chocolate Shot*

Ingredients:
3 tablespoon coconut milk
1 ½ tablespoon cocoa powder
½ teaspoon vanilla
1 serving of sweetener

Procedure:

Prepare this dessert by adding coconut milk, cocoa powder, vanilla and sweetener. Blend until smooth. Place is a small shot cup.

25. Apple and Honey Chocolate Coated Dessert

Insert a stick to the apple's core. Lightly brush the apple all over with honey. Melt a bar of dark chocolate. Dip the apple with honey on the chocolate. Let it set in the refrigerator.

26. Caramelized Banana on Chocolate Ice Cream

Make a homemade chocolate ice cream. Place in the freezer. Over low heat, place 2 pieces bananas, peeled and cut into small pieces, into the pan. Add 1 tablespoon maple syrup or honey until it thickens a little. Remove from heat, and allow to cool for several minutes. Place on top of the ice cream.

27. Chocolate Filled Peaches
Melt a bar of your favorite Paleo dark chocolate bar. Get 3-5 peaches, peeled and cut into halves. Remove the inner core and fill it with the melted chocolate instead. Set in the refrigerator for 30 minutes.

28. Banana and Chocolate

Get a ripe banana and quarter it but do not remove the peel. Pour a tablespoon of melted chocolate over the banana. Add chocolate chips on the side.

29. Strawberry And Chocolate Combo

Using a double broiler, melt a bar of dark chocolate. Cut the strawberry into halves and core the center. Place the melted chocolate into the center.

30.   *Minty Black Forest Shake*

This is a combination of the Black Forest Shake Place and Minty Chocolate Shake.

Ingredients:
2 tablespoon unsweetened cocoa powder
1 cup pitted cherries
1 cup coconut milk
5-6 pieces mint leaves

Procedure:
Just blend the following: unsweetened cocoa powder, pitted cherries, coconut milk and mint leaves. Whir until smooth. You may serve it with nuts or chocolate chips on top.

31.   *Coffee and Coconut Sweets*

Ingredients:
½ cup coconut butter
2 tablespoon 100% cocoa powder
1 tablespoon ground coffee
½ teaspoon honey
1 tablespoon coconut flakes

Procedure:
Melt coconut butter and add 100% cocoa powder, ground coffee, honey, and coconut flakes. Mix well. Evenly grease1 tablespoon coconut oil on the cups of the ice cube tray and place the mixture into each cup. Freeze for 4 hours and take out of the freezer 15 minutes before serving.

Chapter 3 – Baked Chocolate Goodness

Although there were no ovens yet during the Stone Age, all the ingredients here are prehistoric.

1.   *Choco Cookies*

Ingredients:
1 ½ cups almonds
¼ teaspoon baking soda
¼ teaspoon sea salt
½ cup chocolate chips

2 tablespoon coconut oil
½ teaspoon vanilla
½ cup maple syrup
1 egg

Procedure:
In a bowl, combine the following ingredients: 1 ½ cups almond, ¼ teaspoon baking soda, ¼ teaspoon sea salt and ½ cup chocolate chips. In a separate bowl, mix the following: 2 tablespoon coconut oil, ½ teaspoon vanilla. ½ cup maple syrup, 1 egg. Combine the two mixtures and let the batter stay in the refrigerator for 30 minutes.

While waiting for the batter, line the baking sheet with parchment paper. The oven should be preheated to 350°F. Place the batter onto the sheet according to the size of the cookies that you like. Bake for 5 minutes. Take the baking sheet out of the oven and flatten each cookie. Put the baking sheet back for another 5 minutes. Let it cool before serving.

2.   *Beets and Banana Brownie*

Ingredients:
2 red cooked beets
2 eggs
½ cup chocolate protein powder
½ cup unsweetened cacao powder
2 bananas
1/3 cup almonds
1 teaspoon baking powder

Procedure:
Preheat the oven to 325°F. Combine the following in the blender and blend – 2 red cooked beets, 2 eggs, ½ cup chocolate protein powder, ½ cup unsweetened cacao powder, 2 bananas, 1/3 cup almonds, and 1 teaspoon baking powder. Pour into an 8" x 8" lightly greased pan. Bake for 30 minutes. It's different and it's good!

3. *Classic Chocolate-Strawberry Bars*

This has many prehistoric ingredients but worth the effort.

Ingredients:
2 ¼ cups almond flour
½ cup coconut sugar
½ teaspoon baking powder
6 tablespoon flaxseed meal
¼ teaspoon sea salt
2/3 cups arrowroot powder

6 tablespoon coconut oil, melted
3 tablespoon coconut milk
2 teaspoon vanilla extract

½ cup dark chocolate chips
½ cup fresh cut strawberries
1 tablespoon fresh lemon juice
Handful chopped almonds (optional)

Procedure:
Preheat the oven to 350°F. Combine in a bowl 2 ¼ cups almond flour, ½ cup coconut sugar, ½ teaspoon baking powder, 6 tablespoons flaxseed meal, ¼ teaspoon sea salt and 2/3 cups arrowroot powder. In a separate bowl, whisk the following: 6 tablespoons melted coconut oil, 3 tablespoons coconut milk and 2 teaspoons vanilla extract. Mix together the wet and dry ingredients using a gloved hand. This will form soft dough. Take note not to over mix this.

Reserve ½ cup of dough to be used later. Place the remaining dough on an 8" x 8" baking pan lined with parchment paper. Top with ½ cup dark chocolate chips. Cover the chips with fresh cut strawberries. Drizzle with 1 tablespoon fresh lemon juice and then drizzle with the extra dough plus an extra handful of almonds. Bake the dough for 20 minutes then lower the heat to 325°F and then bake for another 10 minutes. It should turn into a beautiful golden color crumble bar. Cut and serve.

4.   *Choco Chip Cookies*

Ingredients:
¾ cup almond flour
¼ cup coconut flour
1/4 teaspoon plus 2 servings of sweetener
½ cup chopped nuts
2 teaspoon baking powder

5 tablespoon coconut butter
1 teaspoon vanilla extract
½ tablespoon honey

Procedure:
Preheat the oven to 350°F. Combine all the dry ingredients in a bowl: ¾ cup almond flour, ¼ cup coconut flour, ¼ teaspoon plus 2 servings of sweeteners, ½ cup chopped nuts and 2 teaspoons baking powder. In a separate bowl, combine all the wet ingredients which are 5 tablespoons coconut butter, 1 teaspoon vanilla extract and ½ tablespoon honey. Combine the wet and dry ingredients until a dough is formed.

Using a small scooper, shape the dough into balls and place them three inches away from each other on the parchment paper baking pan. Flatten them with your hand and bake. Oven time will vary but it is usually around 10-15 minutes or until brown. Serve immediately.

5.   *Fudgy Bars*

Ingredients:
2 cups almond flour
½ cup flaxseed meal
½ teaspoon sea salt
½ cup coconut sugar
2 teaspoon cinnamon powder (optional)
1/3 cup chocolate chunks

1 egg
1 tablespoon vanilla extract
1 cup pumpkin puree

Procedure:
Preheat the oven to 350°F. Mix the following ingredients in a bowl – 2 cups almond flour, ½ cup flaxseed meal, ½ teaspoon sea salt, ½ cup coconut sugar, 2 teaspoon cinnamon powder and 1/3 cup chocolate chunks. In a separate bowl, whisk one egg, 1 tablespoon vanilla extract and 1 cup pumpkin puree. Mix the dry and wet ingredients. Take note not to over mix because it causes extra oiliness. Spread into a lightly greased baking pan. Bake around 25 minutes.

6.   *Choco Banana Surprise*

Ingredients:
2 over ripe bananas
3 beaten eggs
¼ cup coconut oil
½ cup almond butter
3 tablespoon coconut flour
½ teaspoon baking soda ¼ teaspoon salt

1/3 cup mini chocolate chips

Procedure:
Preheat the oven to 350°F. Mash 2 over ripe bananas. Add 3 beaten eggs, ¼ cup coconut oil, ½ cup almond butter, 3 tablespoons coconut flour, ½ teaspoon baking soda and ¼ teaspoon salt. Mix thoroughly until a batter is formed. Fold in 1/3 cup mini chocolate chips. Pour the batter into the baking pan and spread evenly. Bake for 15-20 minutes. Let it cool. Cut into squares.

7.   *Choco Cake*

Ingredients:
7.8 ounces dark chocolate
5 egg, separated
4.2 ounces coconut sugar
5.3 ounces grams almond meal
1 shot coffee
¾ cup raspberries

Procedure:
Preheat the oven to 350°F. Melt 220 grams dark chocolate and let cool. Set aside. In a bowl, whisk 5 egg whites and add 120 grams coconut sugar. Fold half of this mixture into the egg yolks. Continue to fold the egg whites mixture into the chocolate and then lastly, fold it with the remaining half of the egg white mixture. Gently fold through 150 grams almond meal plus the 1 shot of coffee and about ¾ cup raspberries. Bake for 30-40 minutes.

8.   *Choco Muffins*

Ingredients:
½ cup raw pecans, chopped
½ cups almond flour
½ teaspoon ground cinnamon
½ teaspoon salt
1 ½ teaspoon baking soda
1 ½ cups banana
1 egg
1 tablespoon honey
3 tablespoon coconut oil
3 tablespoon coconut cream
½ cup chocolate chips

Procedure:
Preheat the oven to 350°F. In a bowl, place chopped ½ cup raw pecans, 1 ½ cups almond flour, ½ teaspoon ground cinnamon, ½ teaspoon salt and 1 ½ teaspoon baking soda. Set aside. Put in the blender and whir 1 ½ cups bananas, 1 egg, 1 tablespoon honey, 3 tablespoons coconut oil and 3 tablespoons coconut cream. Mix this with the dry ingredients. Fold in the chocolate chips. Place the batter in muffin cups and bake for approximately 15 minutes.

9.   *Chocolate with banana*

Ingredients:
2 cups almond butter
3 eggs
1 cup honey
1 tablespoon vanilla
½ teaspoon sea salt
1 teaspoon baking soda
½ cup melted dark chocolate
1 ripe banana, mashed
½ cup chocolate chips

Procedure:
Preheat the oven to 325°F. Make a smooth batter by blending 2 cups almond butter and 3 eggs. Add 1 cup honey and 1 tablespoon vanilla. Mix well. Add ½ teaspoon sea salt, 1 teaspoon baking soda and slowly add ½ cup melted dark chocolate. Fold in a very ripe banana and chocolate, mix well. Bake for 30-45 minutes.

10. *Ultimate Brownie*

Ingredients:
1 peeled and grated white sweet potato
2 eggs
2 teaspoon vanilla
½ cup honey
½ cup olive oil
1 tablespoon gluten free baking powder
½ tablespoon baking soda
1 cup unsweetened cocoa powder
2 tablespoon coconut flour

Procedure:
Preheat the oven to 350°F. Combine in a bowl 1 peeled and grated white sweet potato, 2 eggs, 2 teaspoons vanilla and ½ cup honey. Mix well. Add ½ cup olive oil and 1 tablespoon gluten free baking powder. Mix well again. Lastly, add ½ tablespoon baking soda, 1 cup unsweetened cocoa powder and 2 tablespoon coconut flour. Place in a lightly greased baking pan. Bake for 30-45 minutes. Top with raspberries or chocolate chips or both.

11. *Macaroons*

Ingredients:
¾ cup egg whites
3 tablespoon honey
1 tablespoon vanilla
3 cups shredded coconut

Procedure:
Preheat the oven to 350°F. Beat thoroughly ¾ cup egg whites and then add 3 tablespoon honey and 1 tablespoon vanilla. Carefully fold in 3 cups of shredded coconut (one at a time). Place the mixture on a parchment paper lined baking pan and bake for 15 minutes. Drizzle melted chocolate on top of the macaroons.

12.   *Chocolate Cake with Apricots*

Ingredients:
3 eggs, separated
½ teaspoon cream of tartar
1 cup chestnut flour
½ cup almond flour
½ cup raw cacao powder
½ cup coconut sugar
¾ cup coconut milk
½ teaspoon baking soda
3 ripe, peeled, diced apricots

Procedure:
Preheat the oven to 350°F. In a bowl, mix 3 egg whites and ½ teaspoon cream of tartar until stiff peaks form. Set it aside. In another bowl, mix the egg yolks, 1 cup chestnut flour, ½ cup almond flour, ½ cup raw cacao powder, ¼ cup coconut sugar, ¾ cup coconut milk, ½ teaspoon baking soda. Fold in the egg whites. Fold in 3 ripe, peeled and diced apricots. Pour into a lightly greased pie mold and bake for 30-45 minutes.

Chapter 4 – Drinks for Dessert

These drinks are not just drinks but can also serve as desserts! Try them now!

1. **Chocolate Shake it!** – Place in a blender 6-8 cubes of ice, ½ cup coconut milk, ½ water and 2 tablespoons raw cacao powder and a sweetener of your choice. Blend until the cubes of ice are crushed. It's refreshing and healthy!

2. **Raspberry Frappe** – Combine 1 1/2 cup frozen raspberries, 6-7 pieces mint leaves, 1 teaspoon maple syrup and 1/2 cup orange juice. Blend until smooth.

3. **Smoothie Delight-** Place the following in a high speed blender: 1 cup frozen mixed berries, 1 ripe banana, 1 cup fresh squeezed orange juice, ½ cup unsweetened almond milk, 1 teaspoon honey. Whirl until smooth.

4. **Berry Shake**–In a blender put: ½ cup milk, ½ cup frozen berries. Sprinkle gelatin and blend until smooth. Add sweetener to the taste.

5. **Heart to Heart** – This is very simple but very heart warming. Place sliced red pomegranates on an ice cube tray that is heart-shaped. Add water. Let it freeze. When serving the dessert, place the heart shaped ice into a transparent drink or water.

6. **Paleo Strawberry and Coconut Smoothie** – Put in a blender the following, 3 strawberries, 1 cup coconut milk, 1

teaspoon honey. Whirl until it is smooth and creamy. Place in the refrigerator or serve as is.

7. **Coffee Frappe**–Place in a blender and mix thoroughly the following: ¼ cup brewed coffee, ½ teaspoon vanilla, 1 cup coconut milk, 1 teaspoon maple syrup and 1 cup crushed ice. Ready to drink!

8. **Mango Smoothie** – Blend all these and serve immediately: 1 mango, ½ lime – just the juice, 1 kiwi fruit and 1 cup coconut milk. That's it!

9. **Salted Caramel Shake**–You will need to blend ½ cup coconut milk, 1 ½ teaspoon cashew butter, 1/3 banana, 2 dried pitter dates, a pinch of sea salt, and 1 teaspoon maple syrup plus a couple of ice.

10. **Pineapple Colada** –Place in the blender and whirl the following: 1 cup pineapple juice, 1 cup coconut milk, lime juice, 1 banana and a few ice cubes. Ready to serve!

11. **Paleo Maple Drink** – Place 8 ounces water in a glass and stir in 1 tablespoon of maple syrup. Drink warm or with ice. It's better than soda!

12. **3 Fruit Smoothie** – You will need to blend 1 ½ frozen bananas, 1 cup frozen blueberries and 1 cup frozen strawberries. Add 1 cup coconut milk and 1 cup acai juice plus some ice cubes.

13. ***Watermelon and Lime Combo***- combine 2 cups watermelon, 1 lime (juice only), 1 teaspoon honey and a couple of ice cubes in a blender. Blend until smooth.

14. ***Apple Cinnamon Shake*** - Use the blender to mix the following: 1 cup apple, 1 tablespoon honey, 1 teaspoon cinnamon, ½ teaspoon vanilla and add cashew nuts if you like.

15. ***Banana Drink*** - Place 2 pieces ripe banana, ½ cup coconut milk, 1 tablespoon honey and ½ cup water in a blender. Whirl until smooth and serve with ice.

16. ***Iced Coffee Goodness***– Pour ice over a brewed coffee in a closed container and shake well. Transfer to a glass and serve!

17. ***Fruit Salad Drink*** – Put in a glass 1 thinly sliced strawberry, 5 blueberries, 5 pomegranates and 1 sliced banana. Add ½ cup sweetened coconut milk. Put some ice cubes and serve.

18. ***Banana And Apple Mix*** – Place 1 peeled ripe banana and 1 peeled and diced apple in a blender. Add ½ teaspoon vanilla extract and 1 tablespoon honey plus ½ cup coconut milk. Whirl until smooth.

Chapter 5 – Kids at Work!

Let these kids have fun making their own desserts. Share the memories as you help your children develop a love for cooking and healthy foods too. Maintain safety at all times please. When the chocolate need to be melted, it would be your job. Allow the kids' imagination and creativity to come to life as you let them design their own desserts!

1. ***Chocolate Covered Berries*** – Kids would surely love these! Oh and adults too! Melt a bar of dark chocolate by using a double boiler. The boiling water on the lower boiler and the chocolate on top. When the chocolate is already melted, just dip a clean berry and that's it.

2. ***Pineapple-banana Popsicles***– Allow the kids to pour the following into the blender: 1 6-ounce can of pineapple juice, 1 banana, ½ teaspoon of vanilla and 1 can coconut milk. Let the adults blend this until smooth. Pour into the popsicle shells and freeze. Sometimes, you might need to soak your popsicle tray in a warm water so that they will come out.

3. ***Luscious Looking Popsicle Strawberry***- pour 1 cup of coconut milk, 3 strawberries, 1 tablespoon honey into a blender. Let the adults use the blender until it is smooth. Pour into the popsicle shells. Let it freeze.

4. ***Layered Delight***- Get a container. Fill the bottom with jelly layer (ask you mom to make this). Put the sliced mango on top of the jelly layer. Then follow it up with diced

Paleo cake (ask mom to buy this- they are ready made at your local store). Then place bananas next, then follow it up with 8 ounces coconut cream. Then on top, you can garnish them with some berries, nuts or more mangoes. Decorate as you wish. Set in the freezer and after 2-3 hours, it's ready to be eaten.

5. **Chocolate Popsicle** –Allow the adults to melt the chocolate. Pour it on a kiddie shaped design container then add the popsicle sticks. Place in the refrigerator to set.

6. **DIY Banana Split**–If you have a homemade strawberry or chocolate ice cream, design it with a banana, chocolate chips and maple syrup.

7. **Easter Bunny Fruit Platter** – place on your plate the following: 2 apple slices as the ears of the bunny, blueberries as the eyes, 1 peach sliced in half to serve as the cheeks, and 4 pomegranates lined as a smiling mouth. Eat anytime!

8. **Chocolate Squares** – Ask your mom to melt a bar of unsweetened chocolate using a double boiler. Remove from heat. Stir the chocolate while you add ½ teaspoon vanilla. Place in a pan and let it set in the refrigerator for 30-45 minutes. You can cut into squares using a plastic knife or ask your parents to cut them for you. Alternatively, add chopped nuts or dried fruit into the melted chocolate.

9. **Cake Pops**–Cake on a popsicle stick! Ask an adult to do this for you. You just design it later. The adult will preheat

the pop cake maker. They would also melt ½ cup dark chocolate with ½ cup coconut milk. Add 2 beaten eggs. Mix well. Add ½ teaspoon vanilla extract, a pinch of sea salt and ¼ teaspoon baking powder. Pipe your batter into the pop cake maker by placing it in a ziplock bag with a corner trimmed. Close the lid and cook for 5 minutes. Turn the other side and cook for 2 more minutes. Insert the stick and freeze for 30 minutes.

10. **Pop Cakes with Vanilla Glaze**– After making the cake pops, prepare the vanilla glaze using ½ cup coconut butter, 2 tablespoon honey and ½ teaspoon vanilla in a small glass. Warm this glass with warm water (an adult will do this) and decorate your pop cake with the glaze or you can just dip in your pop cake.

11. **Chocolate Glaze Pop Cake-** Or you may want a chocolate glaze. Ask an adult to melt ½ cup chocolate chips. Then dip or decorate your chocolate glaze. Add maple sugar, if desired.

Chapter 6 – Other Goodies

There are so many things you can try with the Paleo desserts. Here are some more recipes!

1. *Apple Cookies* – Try this yummy dessert.

Ingredients:
1 egg, beaten
1 cup unsweetened almond butter
½ cup honey
1 teaspoon baking soda
½ teaspoon sea sal
½ apple, cored, peeled, diced
1 teaspoon cinnamon
1 teaspoon nutmeg
¼ teaspoon ground cloves
1 teaspoon ginger, grated

Procedure:
Simply combine the following in a bowl: 1 beaten egg, 1 cup unsweetened almond butter, ½ cup honey, 1 teaspoon baking soda and ½ teaspoon sea salt. Mix thoroughly. Add the apple, just half of an apple and diced, 1 teaspoon cinnamon, 1/8 teaspoon nutmeg and ¼ teaspoon ground cloves. Then lastly, the ginger, one teaspoon, grated. Spoon the batter and place into a baking sheet. Try to spread the butter 1-2 inches away from each other. Preheat the oven to 350°F and bake the cookies for 10 minutes. Remove from the oven and let it cool for 10 more minutes. Then it is ready to be served!

2. Very Nutty Cookies

Ingredients:
2 bananas, smashed
1/3 cup coconut flour
¾ cup almond butter
½ teaspoon baking powder
1 apple, cored, peeled, finely chopped
1/3 cup raw walnuts
1/3 cup coconut milk
1 tablespoon cinnamon

Procedure:
Smashed two bananas and add 1/3 cup coconut flour, ¾ cup almond butter and ½ teaspoon baking powder. Mix well. In a blender, put a finely chopped apple and 1/3 cup raw walnut and blend for 20 seconds. Add this to the banana mixture done earlier plus 1/3 cup coconut milk and 1 tablespoon cinnamon powder. Mix thoroughly. Place onto the baking pan, 1-2 inches apart. Preheat the oven to 350˚F. Bake for around 25 minutes. You will have around 20 cookies ready to be served!

3. Blackberry Cobbler

Ingredients:
3 cups fresh blackberries
Honey
1 ½ cups finely ground almonds
2 tablespoon coconut oil
Cinnamon, to taste

Procedure:
Place 3 cups of fresh blackberries in a pie pan. Drizzle a bit of honey on top of the berries. In a separate bowl, mix 1 ½ cups finely ground almonds and 2 tablespoon coconut oil plus add cinnamon according to your taste preference (maybe a pinch or a teaspoon). Mix well. You would expect the mixture to be thick and clumpy. Crumble this on top of the berries and bake for 35 minutes at 350°F.

4. *Mango Ice Cream* – You can use a blender or an ice cream maker here.

Ingredients:
3-5 pieces of mango flesh
½ cup coconut milk
½ teaspoon vanilla

Procedure:
Place 3-5 pieces of mango flesh, half cup coconut milk, ½ teaspoon vanilla. Whirl until smooth and then freeze for an hour.

5. *Truly Almond Cookies*

Ingredients:
1 ½ cups almond flour
¼ teaspoon salt
¼ teaspoon baking soda
1/8 teaspoon cinnamon
2 tablespoon coconut oil
1 ¼ teaspoon vanilla
¼ teaspoon almond extract
¼ cup maple syrup

Procedure:
In a bowl, put together 1 ½ cups almond flour, ¼ teaspoon salt, ¼ teaspoons baking soda, and 1/8 teaspoon cinnamon. Mix very well, there should be no lumps. In another bowl, mix 2 tablespoons coconut oil, 1 ¼ teaspoon vanilla, ¼ teaspoon almond extract, and ¼ cup maple syrup. Whisk well. Combine the ingredients of the two bowls and stir well. Roll into a ball and then place on a baking pan lined with parchment paper. Flatten the ball slightly and then place one whole almond on the center. Preheat the oven to 325°F and bake for 15-20 minutes. Allow to cool and then serve with Paleo tea.

6. *Grilled Bananas*

Ingredients:
4 bananas, quartered
Cinnamon

Procedure:
Quarter 4 bananas (or depending on the number of your guests) and leave the peel on. Sprinkle cinnamon and then grill the open side first for 2-3 minutes only. Flip on the peel side and wait for 2-3 minutes. Serve hot.

7. Grilled peaches

Ingredients:
Peaches (1 per person)
Cinnamon
Pumpkin pie spice (optional)

Procedure:
Slice the peaches in half and remove the pit. Sprinkle some cinnamon to add to taste. You could also try pumpkin pie spice. Grill for 3-5 minutes and then turn on the other side. Grill too within 3-5 minutes. You may add homemade whipped cream if you desire.

8. Vanilla Fruit Dip

Ingredients:
1 teaspoon vanilla extract
1 cup coconut milk
2 ripe bananas
2 teaspoon coconut flour

Procedure:
Put into the blender 1 teaspoon vanilla extract, 1 cup coconut milk, 2 ripe bananas and 2 teaspoons coconut flour. Whirl for 2-3 minutes until smooth. Serve with slices of peaches, strawberries or apples.

9. Fried Apples Dessert

Ingredients:
2 tablespoon coconut oil
3-4 apples, thinly sliced
¼ cup raisins
½ tablespoon cinnamon
2 tablespoon canned coconut milk

Procedure:
In a pan, heat 2 tablespoons coconut oil over medium heat. Add 3-4 apples, thinly sliced. Add ¼ cup raisins for 2 minutes. Then add ½ tablespoon cinnamon and 2 tablespoons canned coconut milk. Stir well and it's ready to be served!

10.   *Coconut Macaroons*

Ingredients:
16 ounces unsweetened coconut
¼ teaspoon cream of tartar
6 egg whites
1 teaspoon vanilla extract
1 cup honey

Procedure:
Cook unsweetened coconut (around 16 ounces) until it turns golden brown in color. In a separate bowl, using a mixer with a whisk attachment, beat ¼ teaspoon cream of tartar and 6 egg whites. Mix until hard peaks form and mixture is glossy. Stir in 1 teaspoon vanilla extract, 1 cup honey and the golden brown coconut cooked earlier. Mold the mixture into little balls and place on the baking pan. Preheat oven at 350°F. Bake for 10-12 minutes.

11. Pancake Special

Ingredients:
4 eggs, beaten
¼ cup coconut flour
¼ teaspoon vanilla
1 pinch nutmeg
1 pinch cinnamon
¼ cup coconut milk

Procedure:
Pour 4 beaten eggs into a bowl. Add ¼ cup coconut flour, ¼ teaspoon vanilla, 1 pinch nutmeg, 1 pinch cinnamon and ¼ cup coconut milk. Cook like the usual pancake by putting oil on a pan and pouring about ¼ cup of batter. Flip to the other side when it turns brown. Serve with honey or strawberry.

12. Nuts about Coconut

Ingredients:
2 cups coconut milk
1 tablespoon cacao powder
10 dates, seeds removed
2 tablespoon coconut cream

Procedure:
Place the following into a blender: 2 cups coconut milk, 1 tablespoon cacao powder, 10 dates with seeds removed and 2 tablespoon coconut cream. Blend thoroughly. Place into a container lined with parchment paper and freeze. Once it sets, you can slice and serve.

13. Caramel Topping

Ingredients:
2 tablespoon hulled tahini
1 tablespoon honey
2 tablespoon coconut milk
½ teaspoon vanilla

Procedure:
Put 2 tablespoons of hulled tahini and 1 tablespoon honey and mix with a fork. Add 2 tablespoons of coconut milk and ½ teaspoon of vanilla. Place on top of your ice cream for a more delightful dessert!

14. Triple Fruit Layer

Ingredients:
3-5 sliced pieces of peaches
Fruit jelly
Coconut cream
1 teaspoon honey
1 mango, sliced

Procedure:
Prepare a container. On the bottom, place 3-5 sliced pieces of peaches. On top of the peaches, layer it up with jelly. Then brush it with a small amount of coconut cream and a teaspoon of honey evenly spread. The next layer is a layer of sliced mangos, followed with coconut cream again. Spread a variety of berries on top. Put in the freezer until it sets.

15. Partner for Muffins

Ingredients:
5 dates
½ cup water
2 ½ tablespoon coconut flour
1 egg
1 ripe banana, peeled
½ teaspoon baking powder

Procedure:
Heat 5 pieces of dates with a half cup water over low heat until the dates break down. Mash the dates and set aside. Blend by use of food processor 2 ½ tablespoon coconut flour, one egg, 1 ripe and peeled banana and ½ teaspoon baking powder. Combine the dates and this mixture. Cook in the oven for 20 minutes. Place this cooked yummy sweet mixture on top of your muffins.

16. Cool Ice Cream

Ingredients:
4 bananas, frozen
4 tablespoon coconut milk
1 teaspoon vanilla

Procedure:
Simply blend 4 frozen bananas, 4 tablespoons coconut milk and 1 teaspoon vanilla and place in the freezer for an hour or so.

17. Paleo Fruit Salad 1

Ingredients:
1 cup kiwi, peeled
1 apple, diced
1 mango, peeled and diced
1 peach, cut in half and pitted
½ cup coconut milk

Procedure:
Place in a big bowl 1 cup peeled kiwi, 1 diced apple, 1 mango, peeled and diced, and 2 pieces peach. Add ½ cup coconut milk. Chill and serve.

18. Paleo Fruit Salad 2

Ingredients:
2 ripe bananas
1 coconut, shredded flesh

Procedure:
Another combination that will suit the palate is this: add 2 pieces ripe bananas and 1 shredded coconut flesh to the Paleo Fruit Salad 1

19. Fruits and Nuts

Ingredients:
3 dates, pitted
2 ripe bananas
½ cup almond butter
½ teaspoon nutmeg
¼ teaspoon ground cloves
½ teaspoon baking soda
½ cup pecans, crushed
½ teaspoon lemon extract

Procedure:
Preheat oven to 350°F. Blend 3 pitted dates, 2 ripe bananas, ½ cup almond butter, ½ teaspoon nutmeg, ¼ teaspoon ground cloves, ½ teaspoon baking soda, ½ cup crushed pecans and ½ teaspoon lemon extract. Whirl until smooth. Scoop the batter and place on the baking pan. Bake for 10-15 minutes. Allow to cool.

20. *Orange Cake Delight*

Ingredients:
2 oranges, peeled
1 banana, peeled
3 eggs
4 tablespoon coconut sugar
2 cups almond meal
1 teaspoon baking powder

Procedure:
Preheat oven to 350°F. Blend 2 peeled oranges and 1 banana. Set aside. Beat 3 eggs and add 4 tablespoon coconut sugar. Mix well. Add to this 2 cups of almond meal, orange and banana mix, and 1 teaspoon baking powder. Pour to the baking tin. Bake for one hour. Allow to cool.

21. Sweet Bananas

Ingredients:
½ cup water
2 bananas, sliced
½ teaspoon vanilla extract
1 tablespoon maple syrup
½ cup cold coconut milk

Procedure:
In a pan, place the following over medium heat. ½ cup water, 2 piece sliced ripe bananas, ½ teaspoon vanilla extract and 1 tablespoon maple syrup. Cook until it thickens. Let it cool for 10 minutes. Pour ½ cup cold coconut milk and then serve.

22. *Paleo Refrigerator Cake*

This recipe is very similar to the usual refrigerator cake but with a touch of the Paleo ingredients.

Ingredients:
Paleo cake
1 mango, sliced
Coconut cream

Procedure:
Place a layer of homemade Paleo sponge cake (or you can buy this) onto the bottom of a container. Next, make a layer of sliced mango. Pour coconut cream on top and spread evenly. Layer again with the remaining sponge cake. On top, you can decorate your refrigerator cake with different berries.

23.   *Fudgy Espresso Brownie*

Ingredients:
1 cup cocoa or cacao powder
5 walnut pieces
1 cup strong expresso

Procedure:
Blend 1 cup of cocoa powder and 5 pieces of walnuts. Add a cup of strong espresso. Whirl in a blender. After they are totally blended, roll these into small balls. Coffee and brownie all in one!

24.   *Upside Down Banana Cake*

Ingredients:
2 tablespoon coconut butter, melted
2 tablespoon coconut sugar
1 teaspoon cinnamon
1 banana, sliced
2 eggs
1/3 maple syrup
¼ cup unsweetened coconut milk
1 teaspoon vanilla extract
½ teaspoon baking soda
1 teaspoon apple cider vinegar
1 small banana, mashed
1/3 cup coconut flour

Procedure:
Preheat oven to 350°F. Put 2 tablespoon melted butter on the baking pan. Sprinkle 2 tablespoon coconut sugar evenly on top of the melted butter. Then sprinkle 1 teaspoon cinnamon. Layer one sliced banana next. In a bowl, mix 2 eggs, 1/3 maple syrup, ¼ cup unsweetened coconut milk, 1 teaspoon vanilla extract, ½ teaspoon baking soda, 1 teaspoon apple cider vinegar and 1 small mashed banana. Mix well. Add 1/3 cup coconut flour. There should be no lumps. Place on the pan and bake for approximately 25 minutes. Slice and serve upside down.

25.   *Apple Cinnamon Cake*

Ingredients:
½ cup almond flour
¼ cup arrowroot starch
1/3 cup coconut sugar
2 tablespoon almond
1 tablespoon cinnamon
1 teaspoon baking powder
¼ teaspoon salt
1 tablespoon almond or coconut butter
2 eggs, beaten
½ cup coconut milk
1 teaspoon vanilla
1 cup apple, grated

Procedure:
Place in a food processor the following dry ingredients: ½ cup almond flour, ¼ cup arrowroot starch, 1/3 cup coconut sugar, 2 tablespoons flour, 1 tablespoon cinnamon, 1 teaspoon baking powder and ¼ teaspoon salt. Whirl for a few times. Add 1 tablespoon butter and whirl. In a bowl, mix 2 beaten eggs, ½ cup coconut milk, 1 teaspoon vanilla. Add 1 cup grated apple and stir. Add to the food processor. Pour the mixture into the baking pan and bake for 30 minutes. Serve as it is or add a topping like the next recipe.

26. *Apple Cinnamon Cake with Walnut Topping*

Ingredients:
1 ½ cups walnuts
½ cup coconut flour
4 tablespoon coconut butter
2 tablespoon coconut sugar
Pinch of salt
1 tablespoon cinnamon

Procedure:
Make a topping by mixing the following ingredients: 1 ½ cups walnuts, ½ cup flour, 4 tablespoons melted butter, 2 tablespoon coconut sugar, a pinch of salt and 1 tablespoon cinnamon. Whirl in the food processor and then sprinkle on top of your apple cinnamon cake.

27. Simply Orange Cake

Ingredients:
2 oranges
6 eggs, beaten
10.5 ounces almond meal
3.5 ounces coconut syrup
1 teaspoon baking soda

Procedure:
Preheat the oven to 325°F. Boil 2 oranges in a saucepan for about 2 hours. Blend thoroughly the oranges and 6 beaten eggs in a processor. Add 10.5 ounces almond meal, 3.5 ounces coconut syrup and 1 teaspoon baking soda. Mix well and then place batter on the baking pan and bake for 45 minutes.

28. Peanut Butter Delight

Ingredients:
5 tablespoon sunflower seed butter
1 tablespoon honey
1 tablespoon coconut oil
1 tablespoon flaxseed meal
1 tablespoon vanilla
¾ cup almond flour
Pinch of salt
¼ cup chocolate chips
1 tablespoon cacao butter
Chopped almonds

Procedure:
In a large bowl, mix with your gloved hand the following ingredients: 5 tablespoons sunflower seed butter, 1 tablespoon each of honey, coconut oil, and flaxseed meal, 2 tablespoon vanilla, ¾ cup almond flour and a pinch of salt. Roll the dough into a ball and refrigerate for 30 minutes. Melt ¼ cup chocolate chips and 1 tablespoon cacao butter. Dip the balls into this and top with chopped almonds. Refrigerate until firm and then serve!

29. Raw Brownie Bites

Ingredients:
1½ cups walnuts
Pinch of salt
1cup pitted dates
1 teaspoon vanilla
1/3 cup unsweetened cocoa powder

Procedure:

Add walnuts and salt to a blender or food processor. Mix until the walnuts are finely ground. Add the dates, vanilla, and cocoa powder to the blender. Mix well until everything is combined. With the blender still running, add a couple drops of water at a time to make the mixture stick together. Using a spatula, transfer the mixture into a bowl. Using your hands, form small round balls, rolling in your palm. Store in an airtight container in the refrigerator for up to a week.

30. Paleo Chocolate Cupcakes

Ingredients:

4 eggs

1/2 cup honey

1/3 cup coconut flour

1/4 cup cacao powder

1/2 teaspoon baking soda

1/4 cup coconut oil (melted in microwave)

1/4 cup cacao butter (melted in microwave)

For topping:

1 can coconut cream (chilled in fridge overnight)

Honey (optional)

1/4 cup jam or coulis (See my easy jam recipe here.)

Cacao nibs to decorate.

Procedure:

Heat the oven to 170°Celsius (338°F). Grease 10 muffin pans with coconut oil. Beat eggs and honey with electric beaters. Add coconut flour, baking soda and cacao powder. Beat well. Add melted coconut oil, cacao butter and mix. Spoon mixture into 10 greased muffin pans. Bake for 12-15 minutes until risen and top springs back.

Cool in pans. Beat the solid coconut cream with electric beaters until creamy. Add honey to taste if you wish. Pipe coconut cream onto top of cakes. Drizzle with jam or coulis.

31. Chocolate "Peanut Butter" Ice Cream with Chocolate Shell

Ingredients:
For the ice cream

2 (14 ounce) cans coconut milk

3 tablespoons unsweetened cocoa powder

⅓ cup raw honey

1 teaspoon instant coffee (I used ground coffee)

⅛ teaspoon cinnamon

Pinch of salt

¼ cup sunflower seed butter (or other nut butter)

For the chocolate shell

¼ cup coconut oil, melted

1 tablespoon unsweetened cocoa powder

1 tablespoon sunbutter (or other nut butter)

2 tablespoons raw honey

½ teaspoon vanilla extract

Pinch of salt

Procedure:

Place a saucepan over medium heat and add all ice cream ingredients to it, except for the sunflower seed butter. Stir until cocoa powder is completely broken down and ingredients are smooth. Place saucepan in the freezer until cool. Mine took about an hour. Pour ice cream ingredients in your ice cream maker and turn on. When ice cream is almost done mixing, pour in the sunflower seed butter directly into the ice cream maker to churn with your chocolate ice cream. While ice cream is churning, place the chocolate shell ingredients in a bowl and in the microwave for about 30 seconds until everything is mixed. Whisk together until smooth. When ice cream is done churning, place in bowl and bowl chocolate shell on top!

32. Strawberries& Cream Ice Cream with Almond Butter Crisp

Ingredients:

For the Ice Cream:

1 can full fat coconut milk

3 tablespoon honey

2 tablespoon vanilla

1 cup fresh strawberries, cut into fourths

For the crisp:

1/3 cup almond flour

3 tablespoon sunflower seed butter (or almond butter)

1/2 teaspoon vanilla

1 tablespoon honey

salt to taste

Procedure:

For the ice cream:

Combine coconut milk, honey, and vanilla together in a small saucepan over medium heat and stir until ingredients are well combined (just a few minutes). Transfer milk mixture to a small bowl and place in the freezer for two hours. Next, add strawberries to a small saucepan and bring to a low boil. Turn heat to medium-low and allow to cook until they start breaking down into a sauce-like mixture, leaving small chunks. Place strawberries in refrigerator while the ice cream hardens.

For the crisp:

Combine all ingredients and mix until you get a "crumble" consistency. Place crisp in refrigerator until ready to use. After two hours, place milk mixture into your ice cream maker along with the strawberries and use as directed. When ice cream is ready, scoop and serve with crisp sprinkled on top.

33. Paleo White Chocolate

Ingredients:
1/4 cup of raw cacao butter, melted

1 teaspoon maple sugar

1 teaspoon of vanilla powder

2 ounces coconut milk powder

Tiny pinch of salt

1 teaspoon cacao nibs (optional for inside your chocolates)

Procedure:

Melt your raw cocoa butter in a glass bowl over a double boiler on your stove set to low (raw cocoa melts at 93 degrees, don't burn it). Once melted, transfer to another bowl and add the remaining ingredients. Whisk well ensuring there are no lumps left and everything is incorporated. Transfer to a blender or a food processor and run it to get it as smooth as possible. Pour into your chocolate molds or silicon cups and place in the freezer for at least an hour. Remove and serve or chop them up and add them to chocolate chip cookies or muffins

34. Paleo Chocolate Chip Pizookie

Ingredients:

2 cups sifted blanched almond flour
1/2 teaspoon baking soda
1/4 teaspoon sea salt
1 cup Enjoy Life Mini Chocolate Chips (soy free, dairy free)
1 organic cage-free egg
1/3 cup raw honey (melted)
1/4 cup coconut oil (melted)
1/2 teaspoon vanilla Extract

Procedure:

Preheat oven to 350 °F. Grease your mini 6″ cast iron skillets. In a large bowl, mix together the almond flour, baking soda, and salt with a fork. Add the chocolate chips to the dry mixture and combine. In a small separate bowl, mix the wet ingredients together, honey, coconut oil, vanilla extract, and egg. You may need to heat the honey and coconut oil in order to liquefy them, remember to heat before you add the egg. Stir the wet ingredients into the dry until evenly mixed. Let the dough chill in the fridge for at least 30 minutes. Then fill both skillets evenly with dough. Bake for 30-35 minutes or until a toothpick comes out clean. Garnish with coconut milk ice cream and enjoy!

35. Blueberry Mango Muffins

Ingredients:

3 eggs

3 tablespoon honey

2 tablespoon coconut oil, melted

2 tablespoon coconut milk

1/4 teaspoon salt

1/4 teaspoon vanilla

1/4 teaspoon baking powder

1/4 cup coconut flour

1/2 cup diced mango

1/2 cup blueberries

Procedure:

Preheat oven to 400°F. Mix together your eggs, honey, coconut oil, coconut milk, salt and vanilla. Sift together your baking powder and coconut flour and then combine with your wet ingredients. Mix your batter well and then fold in your diced mango and blueberries. If not, divide your batter into 9 muffin tins and bake for 20 minutes or until done.

36. Dark Chocolate Fudge Pops

Ingredients:
1¼ cups coconut milk
2 egg yolks
½ cup maple syrup or honey
Dash of sea salt
1½ teaspoons unflavored gelatin
1 teaspoon vanilla extract
2 ounces unsweetened chocolate, roughly chopped

Procedure:

Soften the gelatin by placing it in a small bowl with the vanilla extract. Warm the coconut milk over medium-high heat for 6-7 minutes, being careful not to let it boil. Whisk the egg yolks, maple syrup, and salt in a small bowl. Slowly pour the hot coconut milk into the egg mixture, whisking continuously to temper the eggs. Pour the entire liquid mixture back into the pan, and continue cooking over medium high heat for 6-8 minutes while stirring constantly. You don't want this mixture to boil and it should be thick enough to coat the back of a spoon. Pour the softened gelatin and vanilla into the pan and whisk vigorously until the gelatin has completely dissolved, about 2 minutes. Remove from heat, and pour the mixture into a glass bowl. *If you notice a few small lumps, pass it through a mesh strainer prior to pouring it into the bowl.* Stir in the chopped chocolate until it is incorporated and smooth, then let the pudding cool for 20 minutes at room temperature. Pour the pudding into popsicle molds and freeze for at least 6 hours until solid.

37. Banana Split Ice Cream

Ingredients:
2 cups half & half
1 cup cream
1/8-1/4 teaspoon. Organic KAL Stevia* or sweetener of choice (to taste)
2 teaspoon. pure vanilla extract

Add-Ins:
1 small banana, thinly sliced
1/4 cup crushed and drained pineapple
1/2 cup chopped pecans
1 cup sliced strawberries
1/2 cup cherries, pitted and sliced (optional)
1/4 cup chopped 80% cocoa chocolate bar (optional)
1/2 cup toasted coconut flakes for garnish

Procedure:

In a medium bowl, blend dairy, vanilla and sweetener. It's as simple as that. Follow your ice cream maker's instructions to freeze ice cream mixture. If your ice cream maker allows, during the last few minutes, add your fruits, nuts, and other yummy extras, or fold them in once ice cream is almost frozen before transferring. Transfer the ice cream into a freezer safe bowl, and freeze for at least one hour to set ice cream. Top with coconut. To toast coconut flakes: Place coconut flakes (or chips) into frying pan. Toast over medium heat, stirring frequently to prevent them from burning. Allow coconut to brown slightly, but NOT burn.

38. Sweet Spinach Pie with Basic Paleo Almond Crust

Ingredients:
For the pie crust:

1 cup ground almonds (almond flour)

1 tablespoon coconut flour

1 tablespoon coconut oil

1 egg

Pinch of sea salt

For the spinach filling:

300g fresh spinach leaves (1 cup cooked)

4 eggs, separated

1 cup ground almonds (almond flour)

2 tablespoons coconut flour

1 cup coconut sugar

1 teaspoon rosewater

Pinch of sea salt

Procedure:

For the crust:

In a mixing bowl, knead all the ingredients together until a dough is formed. With your hands, press the dough into a pie plate, bottom and sides (I used a 6-inch round plate). Set aside.

For the spinach filling:

In a medium-sized pot, place the spinach and about 1 cup of water. At medium heat, bring to a boil, and cook about 5 minutes. Reduce the heat to low and cook an additional 5 minutes. Turn heat off and allow to cool in the pot with water. Once the spinach is cool, drain into a colander and press the spinach to remove all of the water. I pressed it with the back of a spoon. Put the spinach, egg yolks, rosewater and sea salt into a food processor. Pulse until a puree is formed, about 1 minute. Add the almond four, coconut flour and sugar and pulse again until everything is well incorporated. Pour the dough into a mixing bowl. Beat the egg whites until stiff peaks form. Fold the egg whites into the spinach mixture. Mix well until no white is visible. Pour the spinach filling into the pie crust. Bake at 180°C (350°F) for 35-45 minutes, or until an inserted toothpick comes out dry.

39. Grilled Peaches with Coconut Cream

Ingredients:
3 medium ripe peaches, cut in half with pit removed
1 teaspoon vanilla
1 can coconut milk, refrigerated
1/4 cup chopped walnuts
Cinnamon (to taste)

Procedure:

Place peaches on the grill with the cut side down first. Grill on medium-low heat until soft, about 3-5 minutes on each side. Scoop cream off the top of the can of chilled coconut milk. Whip together coconut cream and vanilla with handheld mixer. Drizzle over each peach. Top with cinnamon and chopped walnuts to garnish.

40. No-Bake Mini Pumpkin Bites

Ingredients:

FOR CRUST:

1 cup hazelnuts

1/2 cup raw pumpkin seeds

8 date, pitted

1 tablespoon coconut oil

1 tablespoon REAL maple syrup or raw honey

2 pinches of Celtic sea salt

FOR FILLING:

1 cup cooked pumpkin puree

1/2 cup coconut butter

2 tablespoon coconut oil

3 tablespoon REAL maple syrup or raw honey

1/2 teaspoon vanilla extract

1/4 teaspoon cinnamon powder

1/4 teaspoon ginger powder

1/8 teaspoon allspice

1/8 teaspoon clove powder

FOR CHOCOLATE DRIZZLE:

2 tablespoons coconut butter

2 tablespoons coconut oil

2 tablespoons raw cacao

3 tablespoons REAL maple syrup or raw honey

Pinch or 2 of salt

Procedure:

To make the crust: Line mini muffin tins with unbleached mini paper liners. Process all crust ingredients in a food processor until well combined and resembles a coarse flour. Spoon 1 and 1/2 teaspoon of mixture into each of the 24 mini cups. Use your thumb to press down mixture firmly to create a solid bottom layer for these cute little yummies. Place in freezer to harden.

To make filling: Melt coconut butter and coconut oil in a double boiler. Remove from heat and add rest of filling ingredients. Go ahead and mix it up real good here until creamy smooth. Remove crusts from freezer and spoon about 3/4 TBS of filling over your prepared crusts. Return to freezer to harden, at least 2 hours.

To make chocolate drizzle: Once mini bites have hardened, gently melt coconut butter and coconut oil in a double boiler. Remove from heat and add rest of drizzle ingredients. Allow to cool slightly to thicken. Pour into small plastic bag, cut a TINY hole in the corner, and drizzle over treats in any fashion that you want.

Now it's time to enjoy these amazing delights. Store leftovers in freezer as they are best cold.

41. *Chocolate Hazelnut Cups*

Makes about 16-18 cups.

Ingredients:

Two 10 ounce bags of chopped hazelnuts (or almonds, or any nut)

One 10 ounce bag of dark chocolate chips

Two tablespoons of coconut oil--one for the chocolate and one for the nuts

Procedure:

Melt the chocolate over low heat, stirring in a tablespoon of coconut oil once the chips are melted. While your chocolate is melting, add the hazelnuts to a food processor and blend. That's seriously it. It takes a few minutes, but you'll have hazelnut butter before you know it. Throw in a tablespoon of coconut oil for good measure. Spoon some melted chocolate into the bottoms of your candy molds. Add a bit of hazelnut butter. Top it with another spoonful of chocolate. Stick them in the freezer until they've hardened and pop them out. Store them in the refrigerator. Share them with someone you really like.

42. Cherry Vanilla Ice Crème

Ingredients:

2	*14oz. cans Coconut Milk (Full Fat)*
1	*cup raw honey*
1 ½	*teaspoon vanilla extract*
2	*cup fresh Rainier cherries, pitted and diced*

Procedure:

In a large bowl, combine coconut milk, honey, and vanilla and stir well. Chill for 1-2 hours. Transfer to ice-cream maker and process according to manufacturer directions. Add diced cherries to the mixture during the last 5-10 minutes of processing.

43. Apple Pie Caveman Bars

Ingredients:

2 cups dates, pitted

1/2 cup raw macadamia nuts

1/2 cup dried apples

1/4 cup raw almonds

2 tablespoon coconut oil, melted

2 tablespoon cinnamon

Procedure:

Place your dates, macadamia nuts, apples, and almonds in a food processor or really strong blender. Pulse until your dates, macadamia nuts, and almonds are in small chunks and transfer to a mixing bowl. Add in all remaining ingredients. Using your hands mix well to ensure an even coating of everything. Once mixed, using parchment paper, flatten out your mixture to the size of bars your want or you can use individual ziploc bags and form them inside the bag. Place in refrigerator and let cool, then enjoy

44. *Paleo Blueberry and Blackberry Crumble*

Ingredients:

2 cups fresh blueberries

2 cups fresh blackberries

Juice from a fresh lemon

1 cup almond flour

¼ cup chopped walnuts

4 pitted dried dates

½ teaspoon cinnamon

¼ teaspoon salt

¼ cup coconut oil, melted

¼ cup sliced almonds

Procedure:

Preheat oven to 350°F. Place the berries in a 9 inch x 9 inch baking dish, and squeeze juice from half of the lemon over and mix. Press the fruit gently into place and rest at room temperature. In a food processor, combine the almond flour, dates, walnuts, cinnamon, and salt. Pulse until combined. Add in the coconut oil and process on high for 5-10 seconds, or until thoroughly combined. Pour topping into a bowl and mix in the sliced almonds. Sprinkle topping over the berries and lightly press into the fruit with a spoon. Bake for 30-40 minutes, until browned.

45. German Apple Pancake

Ingredients:

6 eggs

1 cup almond milk

3 tablespoon coconut oil, melted

2 teaspoon vanilla

2 teaspoon pure maple syrup

1/4 cup coconut flour

1/2 teaspoon baking soda

1/8 teaspoon nutmeg

2 apples, cored and diced

2 tablespoon coconut oil

2 tablespoon raw organic honey

1 teaspoon cinnamon

1 teaspoon nutmeg

juice of 1/2 lemon

handful of crushed pecans

Procedure:

Preheat Oven to 425°F. In a large bowl, whisk eggs, almond milk, coconut oil, vanilla, and maple syrup. In a small bowl, stir coconut flour, nutmeg, and baking soda. Mix dry ingredients into wet ingredients and beat well to combine, set aside while you prepare the apples. In a small frying pan, heat 2 tablespoon coconut oil and raw organic honey. Stir in cinnamon and nutmeg and juice of 1/2 Lemon and cook for 1 minute. Add in your apples and sauté until all your apples are nicely coated. Evenly divide your apple mixture between 8 ramekins greased with coconut oil and then evenly divide your egg mixture on top of the apples between the 8 Ramekins. Place your Ramekins on a baking sheet and bake for 20 minutes at 425 and then reduce heat to 375 and cook for an additional 20 minutes. Sprinkle with pecans when removed from the oven.

46. Paleo Chocolate Coffee Coconut Truffle Desserts

Ingredients:

1/2 cup coconut butter

3 tablespoons 100% cocoa powder

1 tablespoon ground coffee

1 tablespoon unsweetened coconut flakes

1/2 teaspoon raw honey

1 tablespoon coconut oil

Procedure:

Melt the coconut butter (in a microwave) so that it can be mixed with a fork. Mix in all the ingredients (except the coconut oil) and mix well with a fork. Take an ice-cube tray and pour approximately 1/4 teaspoon of coconut oil into 6-7 of the cups. Spoon the mixture into each cup of the ice-cube tray and gently pat them flat with a fork. Freeze for 4-5 hours. Defrost at room temperature for 15-20 minutes before serving.

47. Fudgy Espresso Brownies

Ingredients:
For the Brownie

6 tablespoons of Pastured Butter

6 ounces of Solid Semisweet Chocolate

2 tablespoons of Packed Coconut Flour (20g)

¼ cup plus 2 Tablespoons of Tapioca Flour (45g)

1 cup of Sucanat or Palm Sugar (165g)

¼ cup of Strong Hot Coffee

¼ cup of Unsweetened Cocoa Powder (30g)

2 Eggs

½ teaspoon of Baking Soda

¼ teaspoon of Kosher Salt

Extra butter for pan greasing

For the Mocha Frosting

¼ cup of Pastured Butter, melted

¼ cup of Pastured Butter, softened

¼ cup of Strong Hot Coffee

¾ cup of Sucanat or Palm Sugar

Procedure:
For the Brownie

Preheat the oven to 350°F. Grease an 8x8 baking pan and line with parchment paper. Ensure eggs are at room temperature. You may run them under warm water for about 10 seconds while shelled. Gently melt the semisweet chocolate and butter in a double boiler. You may use the microwave at 50% heat at 30 second intervals with intermittent stirring. Stir in the coffee and unsweetened cocoa powder. Measure the sugar and coconut flour and add to a food processor. Give a few pulses to make a superfine texture. Sift together the superfine coconut flour, sugar, tapioca flour, baking soda, and salt. Beat the eggs and add the dry ingredients. Beat until combined. Add the rest of the wet ingredients and beat until incorporated. Pour the batter into the lined 8x8 pan. Bake for 25-30 minutes at 350F until a toothpick inserted into the center of the batter comes out clean. When done, remove from the oven and let cool in the pan for at least 15 minutes.

For the Mocha Frosting

Measure the sugar and add to the food processor. Give a few pulses to make a superfine texture. Gently heat the sugar with the ¼ cup of melted butter and coffee until dissolved or mostly dissolved. Refrigerate the mixture for a few hours. It will look terrible at this stage, but don't despair. It is beneficial, but not necessary, to mix every now and then while cooling. When the mixture is cold enough, beat in the softened butter 1 tablespoons at a time on high speed. I find the hand mixer best for this task.

Conclusion

Thank you again for this book!

I hope this book was able to help you to enjoy your sweets without the guilt and without compromise to your health!

The next step is to go out and start buying those prehistoric ingredients at your local grocery stores. Have fun exploring your creativity and finding new ways to enjoy sweets!

In addition, please remember to check out our Facebook page in order to find other resources and upcoming promotions:

https://www.facebook.com/joypublishing

With sincere thanks,

Emma Rose

Preview Of "Paleo Free Diet Guide for Beginners: Over 50 Paleo Free Diet Recipes for Fast Weight Loss and Optimal Health"

Introduction

I want to thank you and congratulate you for purchasing this book!

This book contains everything you might need to know when it comes to getting started with the Paleo Free Diet. It is provided in an easily digestible format that allows you to better absorb the information. There are no complicated explanations about how it works! You'll be given what you need straight up so you won't have to waste time trying to understand exactly what the diet is. Whether it's for your overall good health or to lose a few pounds, Paleo can certainly help you with it. To help you get started, we'll do the same and start you off with 50 of the best Paleo recipes that you can slowly but surely shift your everyday menu to.

It's never easy changing a diet. I often fall into self-pity when I can no longer have the foods I enjoy. Either I feel sorry for myself or I get rebellious and binge and anything and everything. I always knew the value of eating healthy. I could just never bring myself to do it. It wasn't until I had a miscarriage that I got serious about my health. I have made drastic changes that others just don't understand. But the payoff is the weight I've lost and the better health I'm experiencing.

My hope for you is not to be on another "diet." This isn't a restriction diet like Atkins. The goal is to have a lifestyle change.

Lifestyle changes are more sustainable and maintain weight loss long term compared to restriction diets. The change is hard to start but worth it when you commit. The trick is to get the momentum to start.

Thanks again for purchasing this book. I hope you enjoy reading it and eating the recipes from it!

With gratitude,

Emma Rose

Chapter 1 – What Is the Paleo Free Diet?

The Paleo Free Diet is known by many names such as the cavemen diet, stone age diet and hunter-gatherer diet, to name a few. The concept behind this diet follows that of the Paleolithic era before the development of agriculture. Essentially, you consume the same foods that the cavemen used to eat. The focus is on eating food closest to its natural, unprocessed state. The cavemen would gather their food from any source available whether it was wild animals, berries, vegetables, or fruits. As a result, they were strong, fit, and healthy for thousands of years.

This type of diet is still very young, less than fifty years only, but more in depth researches and studies are being conducted to increase the information and knowledge on this diet. The results of previous studies conducted on the Paleo Free Diet reveal the improvement of health to the people involved. This is attributed to the fact that no processed foods and additives are included. The Paleo Free Diet is a diet that works with our genetics – before machinery and processing got involved. Foods that were not available during the Paleolithic time such as dairy products, salt, sugar and grains are not included in the preparation of the Paleo Free Diet.

The modern diet predominately consumed in the Western world is full of refined foods, trans fats, salt and sugar. These ingredients are known to indirectly cause diseases such as hypertension, diabetes, strokes, obesity and other heart problems. The list goes on even further with the increase diagnosis of cancer, Parkinson's, Alzheimer's, depression and infertility. "What an extraordinary achievement for a civilization: to have developed the one diet that reliably makes its people sick!" (Michael Pollen, Food Rules: An Eater's Manual, Penguin Books 2009).

Foods included in the Paleo Free Diet

- Fruit

- Vegetables

- Lean Meat

- Seafood

- Nuts/Seeds

- Healthy Fats (eg. coconut, avocado, nuts and seeds, olive oil, grass fed butter)

Foods NOT included in the Paleo Free Diet

- Dairy

- Grain

- Processed Food

Why not grain?

You may be surprised to see that grains are not included in the Paleo Free Diet. We are accustomed to grains being a part of a balanced diet. However, our bodies are not designed to deal with the nutritional components of grains such as gluten, lectin, and phytates.

Gluten is a protein substance found in wheat, barley and rye. Many people are discovering that their bodies are gluten sensitive and are eliminating gluten from their diet. The most extreme case of gluten sensitivity is Celiac Disease. Individuals with this disease can pick up the minutest trace of gluten and react immediately.

Lectin binds to insulin receptors and can also cause leptin resistance.

Phytates cause minerals to become unavailable during digestion.

Why is dairy a problem?

When purchasing milk, you need to be mindful of the source.

Check out the rest of this book on Amazon

Or go to: http://amzn.to/1jIJUFX

Check Out My Other Books

Below you'll find some of my other books also available:

Paleo Free Diet Guide for Beginners: Over 50 Paleo Free Recipes for Optimal Health & Fast Weight Loss

Paleo Desserts: Satisfy Your Sweet Tooth With Over 100 Quick & Easy Paleo Dessert Recipes & Paleo Baking Recipes

Raw Food Diet Guide: Lose Weight Quickly, Achieve Optimal Health & Feel Energized with the Raw Food Diet & Raw Food Recipes

Clean Eating Guide: Lose Weight Quickly, Achieve Optimal Health & Feel Energized with Clean Eating For Busy Families & Clean Eating Recipes

Alkaline Diet Guide: Lose Weight Quickly, Achieve Optimal Health & Feel Energized with the Alkaline Diet & Alkaline Recipes

Coconut Flour Recipes for Optimal Health & Quick Weight Loss: Gluten Free Recipes for Celiac Disease, Gluten Sensitivities & Paleo Free Diets

Almond Flour Recipes for Optimal Health & Quick Weight Loss: Gluten Free Recipes for Celiac Disease, Gluten Sensitivities & Paleo Free Diets

Wheat Free Diet for Beginners: Lose Weight Quickly, Achieve Optimal Health & Feel Energized with Gluten Free Recipes for Celiac Disease, Gluten Sensitivities & Paleo Free Diets

Detox Diet Guide: Lose Weight Quickly, Achieve Optimal Health & Feel Energized Through the 10 Day Detox

Sugar Detox Guide for Beginners: Lose Weight Quickly, Achieve Optimal Health, Feel Energized & Eliminate Sugar Cravings Naturally

Ketogenic Diet Guide for Beginners: How to Achieve Rapid Weight Loss, Optimal Health & Unstoppable Energy with Ketogenic Diet Recipes

Anti Inflammatory Diet for Beginners: Lose Weight Fast, Optimize Health, Slow Aging, Fight Inflammation, Conquer Pain & Increase Energy with the Anti Inflammation Diet Recipes

One Last Thing...

Source: Wikipedia

If you believe that this book is worth sharing, would you please take the time to let others know how it affected your life? If it turns out to make a difference in the lives of others, they will be forever grateful to you, as will I.

Made in the USA
Middletown, DE
21 July 2017